What Has Ten Legs and Eats Corn Flakes?

What Has Ten Legs and Eats Corn Flakes?

A Pet Book

by RON ROY
illustrated by Lynne Cherry

CLARION BOOKS
TICKNOR & FIELDS : A HOUGHTON MIFFLIN COMPANY
NEW YORK

Clarion Books
Ticknor & Fields, a Houghton Mifflin Company

Printed in the United States of America

Library of Congress Cataloging in Publication Data

Roy, Ron, 1940—
    What has ten legs and eats corn flakes?
    A pet book.
Summary: A brief introduction to the care and feeding of
three small and easily maintained pets.
1. Hermit crabs as pets—Juvenile literature.
2. Gerbils as pets—Juvenile literature.
3. Chameleons as pets—Juvenile literature.
[1. Hermit crabs as pets. 2. Gerbils. 3. Chameleons as pets.
4. Pets] I. Cherry, Lynne, ill. II. Title. III. Title: What has
ten legs and eats corn flakes?
SF416.2.R74   636.08'87   82-1220
ISBN 0-89919-119-3   AACR2

For Robin and Laurel and Buddy   *R. R.*

To Mom and Dad   *L. C.*

Introduction

Pets are fun. You can play with them and talk to them. (Some may even talk back to you!)

Most of you probably cannot have big pets like horses. Some of you may not have room at your house for a cat or dog.

Here are three small pets you can care for quite easily. Even if you are too young to go to school, you are old enough to take care of the pets in this book.

These three animals are all different. But they are the same in some ways, too. They all like to be safe and warm. They eat food you have in your house. And they all like people.

This book is for you and your pet. We hope it helps you to enjoy each other.

One

What has ten legs, eats corn flakes,
and carries his house on his back?

Did you say a turtle? But turtles
have only four legs.

Would you like to see the animal with ten legs?
Just go to a pet shop. Ask to see a land hermit
crab. This drawing is very big. Real hermit crabs
are about the size of a golf ball.

Like all pets, land hermit crabs need someone to take care of them. That someone could be you. Remember these five things and your pet crab should stay happy and healthy:

1. Give your crab a safe home. Use an aquarium. Cover the bottom with gravel. Put in a small tree branch so your crab can climb. Clean your crab's home two times every month. Look on page 44 of this book to learn how.

2. Feed your hermit crab some of the food you like. Put it in a small dish in the aquarium. Try lettuce, bread, crackers, corn flakes, or cookies. Or you can buy special food at the pet store.

Don't be surprised if your crab eats only a little. He'll be fine. And take the old food out every day. Your crab likes a clean home.

3. Keep a small dish of water in your crab's home. This is for drinking. Sprinkle the bottom of his home with warm water three times a week.

4. Put your crab's home in a safe place.
Never put it anywhere near a radiator or air
conditioner. Crabs like rooms that are not
too hot and not too cold.

5. Buy a few extra shells when you buy
your crab. Make sure the shells are bigger
than the one your crab is living in. When
land hermit crabs grow, they move into
bigger shells. Watch your crab try on his
new houses.

Now that you know how to care for your crab, you can have fun with him.

Pick him up gently by his shell. Never pick him up by his legs. And never try to pull your crab out of his shell. That's a sure way to hurt him.

Only very big crabs can hurt you. Read page 42 of this book to learn how to handle your crab.

Hermit crabs are not expensive. Buy two or three and they will keep each other company.

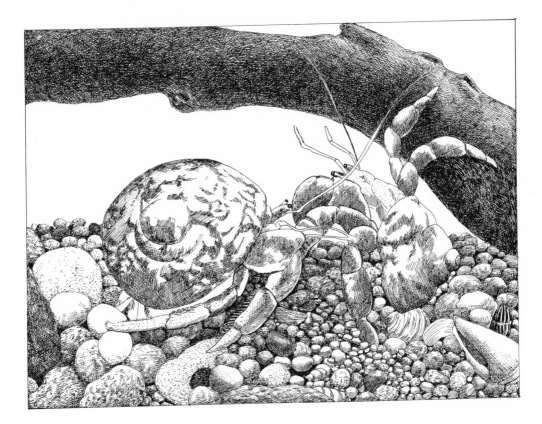

Remember what you should give your crab:

1. a clean and safe home

2. fresh food (Remove the old food every day.)

3. fresh water to drink and sprinkles every other day

4. a room that's not too hot or too cold

5. extra shells and playmates

The only other thing your hermit crab needs is an owner who is kind and gentle. That's you.

Two

What has hands like a squirrel, hind legs like a kangaroo, and a tail like a lion?

Does this sound like a creature from another planet?

It is a gerbil. This is a big drawing. Real gerbils are much smaller. One would fit in your shirt pocket. You can buy a gerbil at the pet store.

Gerbils have soft fur. They are playful and
curious. Remember five things and your pet gerbil
will be your friend for a long time:

1. Gerbils need homes that are safe and clean. Use an aquarium with a screen top so the gerbil will not climb out. Spread pine chips on the bottom. Put in a soft cloth and a short cardboard tube. The gerbil will use these for a nest.

Clean the aquarium every week. Page 44 of this book tells how.

2. Gerbils like crunchy food. Try giving yours corn flakes, rice, peanuts, or potato chips. Put in fruits and vegetables, too. Try lettuce, carrots, celery, grapes, and apples. Be sure to clean out the old food every day.

3. Gerbils need water, too. They will get some
from the vegetables and fruits you give them. But
put in a water bottle also. Ask about water bottles
in the pet store where you buy your gerbil.

4. Your gerbil likes a warm room. He or she will be happy with toys to play with. Try an exercise wheel, blocks of wood, a mirror, or a bell. The gerbil will need a small branch for climbing.

5. Your gerbil would be lonely with no playmates. Never put two males together. They will fight instead of play. If you buy a male and a female, they will mate. You may not be able to care for the babies. Why not buy two females?

If you want to play with your gerbil, make sure she knows you first. Let her walk into your hand.

Then lift your gerbil gently. She will explore your pockets. Her little feet will tickle. See page 42 of this book to learn how to handle your gerbil safely.

Gerbils are very gentle animals. But you must be gentle with them, too. Be a good gerbil owner and remember the five things they need:

1. a home that is safe and clean

2. crunchy foods, fruits, and vegetables

3. a water bottle

4. a warm room

5. other gerbils to play with

Three

What can change its color and even walk up a wall?
This may sound like a make-believe animal, but it is
real.

It is a chameleon. This is a big drawing of one.
Real chameleons are only as long as your hand.
They are friendly to people but like to eat insects
and spiders.

Chameleons can change their color slowly. They
have tiny suction pads on their feet that help them
climb walls. You can buy a chameleon at a pet store.
Here are five things to remember:

1. Chameleons need a safe, warm home. Use an
aquarium with a screen top. Keep the aquarium
near a sunny window. Or keep a small lamp turned
on for a make-believe sun. Chameleons need to sit in
the light, but they need shade, too.

2. Put two inches of damp gravel on the bottom of the aquarium. Set two or three small houseplants in the gravel. Stones and small branches will give the chameleon places to sit. Keep the gravel and plants moist. Sprinkle them every day. Chameleons lap the water off the plants. They will not drink from a dish or bottle. Read about cleaning the aquarium on page 44 of this book.

3. Chameleons eat live insects. They like flies, moths, mosquitoes, and crickets. A five-inch chameleon can eat twenty-five small flies a week. Some chameleons like fruit. Try giving yours a small piece of melon on a toothpick. In the winter, you can buy live insects at the pet store.

4. Chameleons like other chameleons, but never put two males together. They will hurt each other. And never put a big chameleon with a small one. The small one may get eaten.

Ask the pet store owner to help you pick out a friend for your chameleon.

5. Your chameleon will get sick if he is too cold. Is your house warm, even in the winter? If not, ask the pet store owner to help you pick out a small heater for the aquarium. Never put your chameleon near a radiator or air conditioner.

You can take your chameleon out of his home. He will not bite you. He will walk on your hand, a bed, or a table. Tame him by feeding him from your hand. Treat him kindly and see how friendly he becomes.

You will enjoy watching your chameleon change color. Remember these five things he needs to stay in good health:

1. a safe home with sunny places and shady places

2. sprinkles of water every day

3. live insects to eat

4. other chameleons, but never two males or big and small chameleons together

5. perhaps a small heater for the aquarium

Do You Want
to Know More?

Would you like to own one of these pets? Maybe you cannot decide which to buy. They are all fun to watch and play with. Here are more facts to help you decide:

Do you know why land hermit crabs need ten legs? The front pair is for climbing, fighting, and eating. The second and third pairs are for walking. The fourth and fifth pairs come out of the shell only when the crab changes homes. These pairs help hold the crab inside his or her shell.

Did you know that before 1952 there were no gerbils in the United States? Then scientists brought a few here from Mongolia to study. One of the things they learned is that these furry animals can have babies every month! All the gerbils in this country came from those first few, brought here by the scientists.

Do you wonder why chameleons change color? Scientists want to know, too. They have learned that at night chameleons are pale green with white bellies. During the day they may turn brown or darker green. When they are cold or upset, they become gray green.

Sometimes the chameleon will turn the color of a leaf or twig he is sitting on. Sometimes not. Changing color always depends on how the chameleon feels.

How much would these pets cost? In some cities, pets cost more than in others. You can probably buy a land hermit crab, a gerbil, or a chameleon for less than $5.

How much will their homes and food cost? A small aquarium costs $10 or $12. A large one costs $12 or $15. Tops for aquariums cost $3 to $6.

Gravel for an aquarium costs about $2 for ten pounds. Pine chips come in bales. One bale costs about $10 and may last up to a year.

A water bottle for the gerbil costs about $3. A heater for the chameleon's home costs about $8.

If you buy food for your pets, gerbil food will cost about $2 for two pounds. Crickets to feed a chameleon cost eight cents each. A box of food for your crab will cost about $2. It will last for months.

When your pet comes home, you may have more questions to ask.

"How should I hold my pet?"

First, approach your pet slowly and quietly. Make sure he knows you before you pick him up. Let him walk into your hands or scoop him up with your hands cupped. Hold him gently but firmly with both hands. Never pick him up when he is sleeping. This will frighten him, and he will bite you.

If your pet wiggles to get free, put him back in his aquarium. If you drop him, he will get hurt. After he knows you better, he may like to be held longer.

"What if my pet bites me?"

Chameleons cannot hurt you. Land hermit crabs may pinch while climbing. These are gentle pinches.

Gerbils have sharp teeth. If your gerbil bites you, put the gerbil back in her home. Wash the spot with soap and water. Show the bite to an adult.

Why did the gerbil bite? Maybe she was frightened. Wait one day before you pick her up again. Remember, go slowly and be gentle.

"What if my pet gets away?"

The pets in this book can hop or crawl away. Hermit crabs are slow, but gerbils and chameleons can be very fast. If they are tame before you take them out of the aquarium, your pets will probably stay with you. If your pet *does* get lost in your house, close the outside doors and windows. Then search everywhere. If you put food out, he or she may come back to eat.

It is best to make sure your pet does not get away. Finding small pets in big houses can be very difficult!

"Will my pet have babies?"

Chameleons and hermit crabs almost never have babies when they are kept as pets.

Gerbils can have babies every month. You may not want so many gerbils all at once. It takes a male gerbil and female gerbil to have babies.

"Can I go on vacation and leave my pet?"

Hermit crabs can be left for weeks if they have food and water.

Chameleons can be left for two or three days. They need live insects. They need sprinkles of water every other day. Ask a friend to look after your chameleon if you go away for longer than a few days.

Gerbils need daily care. A friend should take care of your gerbil when you go away.

"How do I clean my pet's home?"

Once every day remove any leftover food.

Every ten days or two weeks take everything out of the aquarium. Put the pet in a safe place. Wash everything with warm water. Dry everything before putting it back. Put in fresh pine chips for gerbils.

Once every month, wash everything with a special soap for getting rid of germs. Ask the pet store owner which soap to buy.

"How long will my pet live?"

Gerbils usually live to be about four years old if they stay healthy.

Healthy chameleons can live up to about five years.

Hermit crabs live two or three years, but many have lived longer.

"What if my pet gets sick?"

Many small pets are fragile. That means they can get sick easily. This usually happens because the food is wrong or your pet is too hot or too cold.

If your pet stops eating, never comes out to play, or behaves strangely, he or she may be sick. You should call the pet store. The owner will tell you what to do.

All animals will die someday. If your pet dies, you may feel sad. This book should help you keep your pet alive and healthy for a long time.

Bibliography

After you have finished reading this book, you may want to learn even more about your pet. These booklets and books may help you.

Booklets: You may find these, or ones like them, in the store where you bought your pet.

Chameleons as Pets by Mervin F. Roberts, published by T.F.H. Publications, Inc., Neptune City, New Jersey

Gerbils in Color by Barbara Nippert Monroe, published by T. F. H. Publications, Inc., Neptune City, New Jersey

Land Hermit Crabs by Paul J. Nash, published by T.F.H. Publications, Inc., Neptune City, New Jersey

Books: You might look for these in your library.

The Book of Pets by Stanley Leinwoll, published by Julian Messner, New York

Gerbils: All About them by Alvin Silverstein and Virginia Silverstein, published by Lippincott, New York

Your First Pet: And How to Care for It by Carla Stevens, published by Macmillan Inc., New York

Index

Roy, Ron
What has ten legs
and eats cornflakes?

J

219321